THE

POETESS

COUNTS

TO 100

AND

BOWS

OUT

The Lockert Library of Poetry in Translation

Editorial Advisor: Richard Howard

FOR OTHER TITLES IN THE LOCKERT LIBRARY SEE PAGE 121

THE
POETESS
COUNTS
TO 100
AND
BOWS
OUT

SELECTED POEMS BY

ANA ENRIQUETA TERÁN

A BILINGUAL EDITION

Translated by Marcel Smith

PRINCETON UNIVERSITY PRESS · PRINCETON AND OXFORD

Translations of poems and preface copyright © 2003 by Princeton University Press

Published by Princeton University Press, 41 William Street, Princeton,
New Jersey 08540

In the United Kingdom: Princeton University Press, 3 Market Place, Woodstock,
Oxfordshire OX20 1SY

Library of Congress Cataloging-in-Publication Data

Terán, Ana Enriqueta.

The poetess counts to 100 and bows out : selected poems : a bilingual edition /
by Ana Enriqueta Terán ; English versions by Marcel Smith.

p.   cm. — (The Lockert library of poetry in translation)

ISBN 0-691-09671-6 (alk. paper) — ISBN 0-691-09672-4 (pbk. : alk. paper)

1. Terán, Ana Enriqueta—Translations into English.   I. Smith, Marcel.

II. Title.   III. Series.

PQ8549.T4 A27   2002

861'.64—dc21   2002016923

Sonnets numbered, 3, 5, 7, 18, 19, 23, 25, 29, 31, 35, 36, and 39 in the section entitled
"Sonetos de todos mis tiempos" and the following poems appeared in Spanish in
Casa de hablas, Monte Ávila Editores Latinoamerica, 1991: "A un caballo blanco";
"Música con pie de salmo"; "Saludable visión de este lado oscuro"; "Los sueños";
"Recados al hermano mayor"; "Las águilas"; "Piedra de habla"; "Compromiso con la
alegría"; "Piedrecillas de adivinación; "El nombre"; "La poetisa cuenta hasta cien y se
retira"; "Tercer intento de casa materna."

British Library Cataloging-in-Publication Data is available

The Lockert Library of Poetry in Translation is supported by a bequest from
Charles Lacy Lockert (1888–1974)

THESE TRANSLATIONS
ARE DEDICATED TO MY WIFE

Elizabeth

WITHOUT WHOM NOT

Índice

Contents

DE *Albatros*

DE *Autobiografía en tercetos*

FROM *Albatross*

FROM *Autobiography in Tercets*

Translator's Preface

ANA ENRIQUETA TERÁN is a national treasure in Venezuela, where she was born and has lived most of her life. But she is not yet well known to those who do not read Spanish. That may be—it certainly should be—about to change. English-speaking readers can find an insightful and stimulating chapter devoted to her work in a volume just published by Oxford University Press: *Poets of Contemporary Latin America: History and the Inner Life*, by William Rowe of the University of London. Ana Enriqueta Terán is one of eight poets, all flourishing since the 1950s, considered in depth in the book.

In the Terán chapter, as the focus of his commentary, Rowe offers to English readers the most extensive array so far of excerpts from Terán's poems, together with literal English paraphrase. These excerpts are the fullest demonstration so far, for Spanish readers who do not yet know her work, that this poet writes with extraordinary power and beauty, in an idiom peculiarly her own—lyrical, oracular, sardonic, witty, at once infinitely and pitilessly compassionate, sometimes appearing as exquisitely carved *palo santo* wood, sometimes as surreal ritual flame. And the essay offers to people who read only English some insightful talk *about* this writer's genius. But the literal English paraphrases do not pretend to give anglophones an English equivalent of that genius. That is what this little book tries to do.

The poet was born in 1918, a scion of prestigious families, maternal and paternal, reaching back to Venezuela's earliest history, caught up in the country's political and economic vicissitudes. Two of her mother's brothers were political prisoners during the 1930s, and her own immediate family de facto exiles. She began writing as a young girl, and has been writing steadily and patiently since. She began by emulating the intricately rhymed poems of masters like Garcilaso de la Vega and Don Luis de Góngora. Indeed, all through her career she has written *sonetos* and *tercetos*—this last form being essentially the one Dante used in the *Divina Commedia*. But after living in Paris for a time in the early 1950s, she began working also in free verse strongly influenced by surrealist procedures.

She has to date published a dozen books, the first in 1946, the most recent in 1992, and continues to revise a book not yet in print. She was known in literary circles for more than twenty years before achieving, in the 1970s, national recognition. In November 1989, the University of Carabobo conferred on her the title of Doctora Honoris Causa; in December of that same year she was awarded her country's highest literary honor, the Premio Nacional de Literatura. She served as her country's cultural attaché in Argentina during the Perón era, shortly before her stay in Paris. She has lived also in New York and traveled widely in Europe. Her conversation, like her poems, is tough, acute, sophisticated, and erudite. In her twenties and thirties, she was bewitchingly beautiful—once mistaken for the actress Ava Gardner at the zenith of stardom. Now in her eighties and physically frail (she walks with a cane), she remains a charismatic presence, robust in intellect and imagination, full of charm and wise humor. She continues to write nearly every day, to give readings, and to take part in literary conferences at home and abroad. She ended the last millennium at the University of Salamanca in Spain. She continues to work on her *Autobiografía en tercetos*, which has been evolving for two decades, and which she says must not be published while she is alive. She has allowed me to include four excerpts in this little volume.

Her poems show an extraordinary range and variety, both in form and in substance. Some are meticulously insightful representations of the landscapes and cityscapes that have fed her intelligence and imagination. Some are dramatic character studies of persons, actual and historical. But the center of all this work (the still point, we may say, around which it turns) is an intensely particular female awareness.

I say "female" rather than "feminine" to suggest blood and chyme and womb rather than ideology. The quality, the character, the texture of this awareness is uniquely noteworthy. It registers and bodies forth a subtle, tough, lyrical, politically savvy, unflinching, grittily particular, and yet withal exultant experience of *being* girl, daughter, woman, lover, beloved, wife, mother, grandmother, friend, and determined adversary. All these aspects function as transforming modalities in an awareness at once blessed and plagued by the obligation to turn itself into language other people may feed on.

As a person, in private conversation, Ana Enriqueta Terán is courteous, kindly, and unassuming. But she has no doubt that she is, above all, a *poetisa*—a poetfemale. She accepts the responsibility of being a medium through whom in full dreadful splendor wisdom and beauty, uniquely personal and universal at once, manifest themselves. Poets like her are instruments the universe uses to make us know what being human means. The poems are the evidence. Don't snarl over abstractions. Go inside the poems.

And that brings us to the crux of the matter: Whoever wants to enter these poems must use Spanish as the key. English versions do not—*can not*—replicate the Spanish originals. The anglo idiom is, in its character, radically different from *castel-*

lano, in phonology, morphology, syntax, and lexicon. Moreover, the *castellano* instrument has grown and continues to grow in a distinctive culture, where environmental, familial, social, economic, and political customs have their own un-English contexts. It is not only the names of plants and birds and animals, but the actual plants and birds and animals that are not the same in the two cultures. A Spanish *toro* is not an English bull. An Andalusian *caballo* is not a Clydesdale. This is true in peninsular Spain and Portugal; it is perhaps even truer in the *nuevo mundo*. Thus the complexities of human experience actualized in Venezuelan Spanish belong uniquely to that idiom. This experience has to be translated—transfigured—in order even to appear in an alien tongue. Whatever can be achieved will be—perforce—(in Jacques Derrida's keen phrase) *la trace d'une presence absente*: the trace (like a tern's track in mud) of an absent presence. We cannot touch the actual tern—even if we have in fact seen one. And sometimes the bird is one we've never even heard of. There is no *chenchena* in my experience—or in my dictionary.

Accordingly, the English versions here are not offered as replicas of the Spanish originals. The English versions are intended to be, so far as possible, poems as noteworthy *in their own right* as the originals they derive from. Ideally, a reader who did not know ahead of time should not be able to tell which poem is the original and which the derivation. And yet the simple truth is that the English versions, even if masterworks in themselves, *are* derivations. They start with a provided set of materials—images, thematic concepts, dramatic situations, persons—and with a provided architectural design. If done in good faith, they will correspond, as nearly as possible, with the Spanish poems they emulate.

I say "as nearly as possible," because even at the most elementary level, difficult choices have to be made. In 1997 I delivered a paper at the Universidad de los Andes in Mérida, Venezuela, on the risks and choices in translation ("Riesgos y escogencias en la traducción"), specifically in the translation of Ana Enriqueta Terán. The gist of that paper was printed, without the illustrative examples, in the Universidad de Carabobo's journal *Poesía* in September 1998. The pivotal risk, demanding the hardest choices, in my view, is that translation may become traduction in the English sense: You produce a language that is not English even as it violates the Spanish original. The first choice, accordingly, is to make an authentically English poem.

What it comes down to is diction. Diction is the product of lexicon and syntax. Diction essentially means *just these words in just this order*. The kind of English naturally used by native English speakers relies more on monosyllabic and disyllabic words than Spanish does, and more on direct modifiers than on phrasal modifiers. Thus, English will commonly make the "same" sense in fewer syllables than Spanish. Consequently, though in English the ten-syllable line is standard for sonnets, that line is not a good surrogate for the twelve-syllable line used in Spanish. A better choice, going from Spanish into English, is the eight-syllable English line. If the form is rightly married to the substance in either language, it will not go, without cramp or dilation, into the other. A good Spanish sonnet in the Petrarchan tradition will not turn into a good English sonnet in the same tradition. The translator *cannot* replicate the original. He may be able to make a good English poem that suggests why the original is worth paying attention to.

Accordingly, I take it as a given that originals and translations do not and cannot replicate one other. They may, however, mutually and reciprocally elucidate one another. It is like hearing, say, Bach's *Goldberg Variations* played on a piano and on a harpsichord. Each realization may be beautifully moving, and some ears may prefer one over the other. But each does things the other cannot do, in texture and in timbre, and therefore in esthetic effect. Thus, hearing one may help a listener to hear the other better.

That will be true, I hope, of these two sets of poems. But above all, I hope this little book will stimulate readers to read Ana Enriqueta Terán's poems—as she wrote them. An apt emblem for those poems is the Andean landscape she was born and grew up in—the peaks and valleys and plateaus, the variegated vegetation, the overarching sky, the eagles soaring over coffee and cane plantations, rivers and pueblos, spacious houses and adobe huts—all this suffused with a quality of sunlight and play of chiaroscuro that would have exhilarated Paul Cézanne. There is nothing else quite like it anywhere.

Marcel Smith
Nashville, Tennessee

Acknowledgments

I OWE MANY DEBTS of gratitude for help with this book. To four people I owe particular thanks: to Rosa Francisca Beotegui Commins, the poet's daughter, who in May of 1996 placed in my hands a copy of her mother's book *Casa de hablas* (House Made of Utterance); to the poet herself, whose marvelous conversation gave her poems context; to Jose María Beotegui, the poet's husband, whose generous patience and excellent command of English guided me through some straits in the Spanish originals; and to Thomas Rabbitt, long-time friend and masterful poet, whose keen reading of my English versions saved them from many traductions of our mother tongue.

Gratitude is due to Monte Avila Editores, Caracas, Venezuela, for permission to use poems in Spanish selected from the book *Casa de hablas* by Ana Enriqueta Terán, copyright © 1991 by Monte Avila Latinoamericana, C.A.; and to the poet herself for permission to use those selected from the book *Albatros*, copyright © 1992 by Ana Enriqueta Terán, as well as those from the manuscript of *Autobiografía en tercetos* (Autobiography in Tercets), never before published.

A Note about Sources

THE POEMS gathered here come from three volumes. "De *Casa de hablas* / From *House Made of Utterance*" contains poems from the collection of the same name (Caracas: Monte Avila Editores, 1991), which is a collection of the poet's work to that date. The poems in this first section of the book are not arranged chronologically; rather, they are arranged so as to make, together with the other three sections of the book, a thematically coherent whole. "De *Sonetos de todos mis sientos* / From *Sonnets out of All My Seasons*" contains a dozen poems taken from the thirty-nine numbered parts, which were written between 1970 and 1989: those numbered 3, 5, 7, 18, 19, 23, 25, 29, 31, 35, 36, and 39. Next come six poems culled from *Albatros* (Merida: Universidad de los Andes, 1992). The final section includes four poems taken from the as yet unpublished *Autobiografía en tercetos*. Poems selected for the book include *sonetos* and *tercetos* as well as poems in *verso libre*, short poems as well as longer ones. For reasons of space and proportion, some lovely lengthy sections of the *Autobiografía* were passed over for briefer ones. The poems from *Albatros* follow the order of the book they were chosen from; so too do the poems from the *Autobigrafía*—except that the last poem in this collection is the opening poem of the book it comes from.

My earlier English versions of three poems—"La poetisa cuenta hasta cien y se retira," and two of the *Sonetos de todos mis tiempos* (numbers 5 and 7)—appeared, together with the Spanish originals, in a bilingual volume of the *International Poetry Review* (Spring 1998).

D E *Casa de hablas*

FROM *House Made of Utterance*

« A UN CABALLO BLANCO »

Qué fragor en las crines, qué lamento
de cuello hasta los belfos conquistado,
resbaladas llanuras el costado:
¡caballo blanco por mi solo intento!

Copian sus ojos el paisaje lento
y un árbol en el fondo gime anclado,
los tintes del azul y del morado,
trepan sus ancas, siguen en el viento.

Huye de mí, se pierde en la verdura
de las yerbas crecidas, adelanta
su pecho hasta el poniente y la espesura,

huye de mí como una racha oscura
y blanco desde el pecho a la garganta
en el fondo de mí canta su albura.

« To a White Horse »

What clashing of mane, what keening
of neck bent toward slathery lips,
sleek pastures of flank: horse pure white
because I will it to be so!

Your eyes copy the grave landscape,
a foundered tree quakes at anchor,
tinctures mulberry and skyblue
clamber your haunches down the wind.

You run from me, are lost in green
cresting grasses, steer your breastplate
toward the clashing western thicket;

you run from me, a darkening pool,
and white from breast to stringent gorge
out of my depths your whiteness sings.

« EL NOMBRE »

Como quien escribe una oración y pide en la oración mucha
    humildad
y un extenso aliento para resistir brillo y cercanía de la
    palabra.
Es mi oficio y la frase resulta de arena negra con pespuntes de
    oro.
Y pide en la oración mucha obediencia y la aceptación del
    nombre.
No la firma, sino el nombre completo en los calveros del
    poema:
                            Ana Enriqueta Terán.
                            Ana Terán.
                            Ana Terán Madrid.
Me gusta este nombre. Esta soledad y raro artificio que se
    desprende
de mí hacia la profecía. Que es yo misma recorriendo las
    islas,
el espacio comprendido entre mi desamparo y las escamas,
    anillos
                        y mordeduras del **clima**.

« THE NAME »

As one who writes a prayer and asks in the prayer for great
    humility
and extensive breath to fight off the glitter and immediacy of
    words.
It's my office, the sentence leaping up out of gold-flecked
    black sand.
And in the prayer asks for great obedience and right grasp of
    the name.
No signature except the name entire on the bald dome of the
    poem:
                            Ana Enriqueta Terán.
                            Ana Terán.
                            Ana Terán Madrid.
I like this name. This solitude and rare artifice detached from
    me
on its way to oracular clarity. That it is me myself running
    about over the islands,
space grasped between my helplessness and the scales, rings, and
    snakebites
                    of **all we live and breathe**.

La poetisa cumple medida y riesgo de la piedra de habla.
Se comporta como a través de otras edades de otros litigios.
Ausculta el dia y sólo descubre la noche en el plumaje del
    otoño.
Irrumpe en la sala de las congregaciones vestida del más
    simple acto.
Se arrodilla con sus riquezas en la madriguera de la iguana . . .

Una vez todo listo regresa al lugar de origen. Lugar de
    improperios.
Se niegan sus aves sagradas, su cueva con poca luz, modo y
    rareza.
Cobardía y extraño arrojo frente a la edad y sus puntos de oro
    macizo.
La poetisa responde de cada fuego, de toda quimera,
    entrecejo, altura
que se repite en igual tristeza, en igual forcejo por más
    sombra
por una poquita de más dulzura para el envejecido rango.

La poetisa ofrece sus águilas. Resplandece en sus aves de nube
    profunda.
Se hace dueña de las estaciones, las cuatro perras del buen y
    mal tiempo.
Se hace dueña de rocallas y peladeros escogidos con toda
    intención.
Clava una guacamaya donde ha de arrodillarse.
La poetisa cumple medida y riesgo de la piedra de habla.

« WORDSTONE »

The poetess finishes the wordstone, measure and hazard.
She cuts on the bias through other ages of other litigations.
She auscultates the day and discovers only night plumed with
  autumn.
She bursts, vested in the simplest act, into the congregation hall.
She gets on her knees with her riches in the iguana's lair . . .

Once quite ready, she goes back to the starting place. The abuse
  place.
Disclaimed are her sacred birds, her dimlit cave, her mode and
  rarity.
Cowardice and foreign recklessness fronting the age and its solid
  gold periods.
The poetess responds to every fire, all chimera, knotted brow,
  loftiness
that replicates itself in equal sorrow, in equal wrestle through
  more shade
through a grain of additional sweetness for rank grown old.

The poetess shows her eagles. She is resplendent in their deep
  cloud wings.
She is made mistress of the seasons, the four she-dogs of fair
  and foul weather.
She is made mistress of gravel and scalped land chosen with
  forethought.
She nails a great fiery macaw where she has to get down on her
  knees.
The poetess finishes the wordstone, measure and hazard.

« Compromiso con la alegría »

Cuánta dulzura para adrizar la noche, y este ramo de actinias
hacia piedras lamidas, de consolación;
piedras, fondeaderos de tiempo sur.
De mujer que atestigua vaivén de cefeidas
por entre relampagueos de mangles.
De mujer que ofrece cimófanas, clemátides
solo para restablecer, Islas, el compromiso con la alegría.

« DEAL STRUCK WITH HAPPINESS »

How much sweetness to make right the night
and this clutch of anemones
near thin smooth consoling stones,
stones havens of southern weather.
Of a woman who watches Cepheids quaver
among lightbursting mangroves.
Of a woman who offers cats-eyes and clematis
only, Islands, for the sake of setting right
her deal struck with happiness.

« LAS ÁGUILAS »

El águila
su espléndida costumbre
de sombra absoluta.
La original la nutricia sobre el cielo de los éxodos.
La que respira en las islas amadas.
El águila cerrada del corazón.
El águila abierta y consumada
en el entrecejo de la patria.
Y aquella fija y muy distante, pura miseria
que intuye bordes de Dios, harapos míos y de Dios
y eso **tan libre y solitario** que se expande en la noche.

« THE EAGLE »

The eagle
his splendid habit
absolute shade.
The original manna-giver above the sky in the exodus.
What breathes in beloved islands.
The eagle shut up inside the heart.
The eagle spreadeagled and consummated
in knotted brows of the fatherland.
And that fixed and far-off unalloyed wretchedness
that intuits God's fringes, my rags and God's
and this **so unfettered and solitary** that spreads itself out in
the night.

« SALUDABLE VISIÓN DE ESTE LADO OSCURO »

Es la hija del platero
trae mensajes de los dioses
y ofrenda a ningún dios.

Reconocidos sombra y porte de águila
ceniza, pan en las alforjas salobres,
circunstancia y nueva de futuros éxodos.

Recios merecimientos
como harapos de otoño
sobre su erguida tiniebla.

Es la hija del platero, sus tramos de especias dulces,
sus joyas esenciales olorosas a continentes inmersos,
a doncella de ubres metálicas y cabellera de herrumbre.

Ella será en la noche
lo que es el girasol
en el recinto de los libres.

Hará memoria de reinos y heredades primigenias.
Calzada con lenguas vivas tomará para sí
las anunciaciones y los símbolos. Es la hija del platero.
Oh! Saludable visión de este lado oscuro.

« Fit Vision of This Dark Side »

It's the silversmith's daughter
carries messages from the gods
and an offering to no god at all.

Shadow and aquiline mien given thanks for,
ash, bread in salty saddlebag,
circumstance and notice of exodus to come.

Robust deservings
like autumnal tatters
over your upright ignorance.

It's the silversmith's daughter, her spans of sweet spices,
her essential fragrant jewels for sunken continents,
for damsel with metal udder and long rusty hair.

She will be in the night
what the sunflower is
in forts of the free.

There will be memory of kingdoms and inheritance
    primogenital.
Causeway with living tongues will take for itself
symbols and annunciations. It's the silversmith's daughter.
Oh! Fit vision of this dark side.

« LOS SUEÑOS »

I

Estuvimos y dejamos sombrías constancias:
bellas y muy lejanas novias como aves
posadas sobre piedras oscuras;
Marinos y soldados vigorosamente espaciados en la noche;
lobas de seda escueta y furtiva por el laberinto de los puertos;
musiquillas intermitentes y ojerosas
como luciénagas en el aceite nocturno.
En cambio y delicadamente ofrecidos,
los pulsos numeraciones y comienzos
del gran jadeo nutricio: y algún trasfondo,
orden o contribución de antiguas verdades
al despiadado, fino, secular semblante del odio.

« DREAMS »

I

We were and we bequeathed somber constancies:
lovely and very far-off sweethearts like birds
poised on dark stones;
seamen and soldiers vigorously arranged in nightspace;
she-wolves of raw and furtive silk through the maze of havens;
little musics intermittent and haggard
like fireflies in night oil.
Delicately and on the other hand offered,
throbs numerations and beginnings
of large nutritious panting: and someone beyond the bottom,
order or contribution of ancient truths
to the fine ruthless secular semblance of odium.

II

Esta vez, hicimos el trecho con máscaras ajustadas
a la más pura delicia, al más puro, solitario ademán
de la doncella y su costumbre de planta enlutada.
Alguien de rodillas
                imitando
                        un girasol.
Polifónica abundancia; rítmico ascenso:
el mar con sus millares de sexos azules,
el mar por debajo de la piel del agua.
Esta vez escuchamos los más extraños colores.
Los perfumes
                entraban
                        por los ojos.
Los perfumes olían a música y cabeceos de selva,
a pianos muy jóvenes sobre la desnudez de las islas.
Entonces por qué volver el rostro y acurrucarse de nuevo
en la cegadora, despiadada vigilia.

II

This time we did the stretch with masks fitted
to the purest delight, to the purest most solitary gesture
of the damsel and her customary mournful stance.
Someone a-kneel
                imitating
                      a sunflower.
Polyphonic plenty, rhythmic arising;
the sea with its thousands of blue genitals,
the sea down under the water's hide.
This time we listened to the most alien colors.
The perfumes
                were entering
                      through our eyes.
The perfumes carried a stench of music and of forest nodding off,
of very young pianos above island nudity.
Then why turn your face away and huddle again
in the blinding contemptible vigil.

III

Me decían: "Salta, echa a correr, deslígate,
vuélvete toda hacia la música;
y abandona, olvida tu necesidad, tu nube salpresa
                    en manos agradables
                    natural
                    delicadamente permitidas."
Porque el tacto de los ciegos desnuda el mármol
desecha o mismo ignora ordenados pliegues a semejanza del
      viento;
laguna de seda sobre los muslos
y palpa sonrisa anterior cuando memoriza boca dócil
de raso simple, instantáneo, casi avergonzado
                    si la vergüenza
                    tuviese que insistir
                    sobre la puerta principal
esa de sombras y pulituras inmóviles.

III

They said to me, "Leap, throw yourself into a run, let yourself go,
turn yourself totally toward the music
and abandon, forget your necessity, your salt-cured cloud
                    in agreeable hands
                    natural
                    delicately allowed."
Because the touch of blind folk denudes the marble,
casts aside or even ignores plackets arranged to resemble wind;
silken lagoon over thighs
and a prior smile palpates when it memorizes a satin
mouth, simple, instantaneous, almost ashamed
                    if the shame
                    should have to insist
                    above the main portal,
this one of shades and motionless polishings.

IV

Trozos de tela, trapos heroicos, gavilanes de otra sed.
Hilachas de águila en vez de alma sobrenadando en el fondo.
Yo tenía sueño: "Adiós." Y fue para siempre.
El muchacho, su carnadura de animal ciego
                                    frente a la aridez infinita.
La soledad imita mis gestos, duerme se levanta conmigo.
La soledad, sombra de tu sombra, tierna, perpleja
maldiciente y otrora dulce extranjera.

IV

Pieces of fabric, heroic rags, sparrowhawks of other thirst.
Shreds of eagle instead of soul floating on the bottom.
I was dreaming: "Goodbye." And it was forever.
The boy, his carnality a blind animal's
                              facing limitless drought.
Solitude apes my gestures, sleep gets up with me.
Solitude, shade of your shadow, delicate, perplexes
the illspeaking and formerly dulcet foreigner.

V

Alguna vez la música, su cuchillada infinita;
el color, sus abanicos de mirajes eternos;
la forma
      asida al águila
             que sustituye la constancia.
Los huesos, los huesos de piedra móvil
reverente y asida al secular esbozo del llanto.

V

At some time the music, its infinite gash;
the color, its fans forever mirages;
the form
      seized by the eagle
                  that stands instead of constancy.
The bones, the stone bones motile
reverent and seized by the secular draft of weeping.

VI

El humillado, el joven recuerdo
surgiendo de la manzana irrespirable,
del retablo consagrado al ave de huellas profundas.

Los montes como negaciones de fino borde
y acucioso perfil angélico.

Juzgará el violento a los mendigos de la fábula
ansioso de verbo y luminosas contraseñas.
Temeré el paso medroso
la entrada y salida de los inconsolados
semejantes al mar y bahías silenciosas.
Descenderá como gota de locura el quehacer lento,
la falena del oscuro designio.

Florecerá en cambio la pura, levitada, insondable
expresión de la niña ciega.

VI

The humbled one, the young keepsake
welling up out of the breathless apple,
out of the altar-cross sacred to the bird that makes deep tracks.

Mountains as fine-honed negotiations
and eager angelic profile.

He will judge the violent against fabled beggars
anxious about the word and lucent shibboleths.
I will fear the dreadful pace,
the coming in and the going out of the unconsoled
like the sea in quiet coves.
The sluggish chore will come down like gout from craziness,
a harmful butterfly darkly designed.

On the other hand will blossom the pure, uplifted, unsoundable
blind girl's expression.

VII

Que la costumbre y las cosas del desamparo
obligan la sonrisa de la extranjera
a su florecilla más desolada.

Que el transeúnte ofrece a la desconocida
su animal tristísimo invisible para ambos.

Que la Nación recorta aves oscuras
sobre las fechas memorables
y el sagrado impulso del sueño.

Que el verano trasciende a rosa espacial
a casa única posada sobre un ritmo de colinas
de amantes que atraviesan el cielo,
y la inefable, continua audacia de las banderas
sobre patrias y huracanes profundos.

VII

Let the the abandonment's habit and stuff
obligate the stranger's smile
at her most desolate floweret.

Let the passerby offer to the unknown
his saddest animal unseen by both.

Let the Nation clip dark birds
over memorable dates
and dream's sacred urge.

Let summer come to be known as a spatial rose,
as a unique house poised above a rhythm of hills
for lovers that traverse the sky,
and the unspeakable continuing audacity of banners
over fatherlands and deep hurricanes.

VIII

Elaboramos la medida, la pausa entre alguien
     y el despojado absoluto.
Afuera ladra la bestia de uno mismo
puerta y más allá
hasta alcanzar la madre y seguir pulso apenas
      empujando, cavando de regreso
      impaciente de nada.
Entonces, vivo, o sólo me nutre lo que habla de mí
(no para mí) alguien que me sueña
y no logra darme estatura, ni minuciosa
      bien pulida osamenta:
Afirmación de cal, último refugio del yo
mientras me salgo, me vuelvo humo
me dejo ir más insomne que el alma.

VIII

We work out the proportion, the pause between someone
                              and the plundered absolute.
Barking outside is the beast of the one same
portal and farther away
toward overtaking the mother and following a throb barely
                              thrusting, digging out of the
                              impatient
                              coming again of nothing.
Then I live, or that feeds me only which says about me
(not for me) something that dreams me
but is not able to give me stature, nor a scrupulously
                              polished skeletal frame:
Lime's affirmation, last refuge of the I
while I ooze out, turn into fumes,
let myself go more sleepless than the soul.

IX

San Marcos:
Capítulo 14.
Versículos 51 y 52.

En manos de ellos la vergüenza, el destino inconcluso.
El huyó desnudo. Vívida tangente
sesgo expresado y súbito
                     entre formas y vocablos eternos.
Alguna luz, alguna nación expresamente de rodillas.
Un solo Adiós: el último, solitario ademán.
Mano espacial y en alto para siempre.

IX

St. Mark 14:51–52

In their hands the shame, the inconclusive destiny.
He ran away naked. Vivid tangential
grimace squeezed out and sudden
 among everlasting forms and vocables.
Some light, some nation decisively on its knees.
A lone goodbye: ultimate, solo gesture.
Spacious hand upraised forever.

From *House Made of Utterance*   31

X

Me llevó al sitio de mi padre y sus hirvientes tortugas;
allá la otra mujer
                          besó por última vez mis manos
                                              y no ha tocado flor.
La tarde transcurría entre árboles predilectos y leídos.
Aconsejando el león, incipiente la loba;
un toro, dulce toro me dio un nombre.

"El heredero no debe jugar a ser comido" respondieron.
Pasaron ocho santos,
                          ocho animales de talla verde
                                              y un hermoso hablador.
Cuando por fin abrí la mano cayó su rostro.
No intenté levantarlo; hablaba desde el suelo.

X

She took me to my father's place and his boiling turtles;
there the other woman
                        kissed my hands for the last time
                                and had not touched a flower.
Evening ran across among trees foretasted and read.
Advising the lion, beginning to be wolf bitch;
a bull, a sweet bull gave me a name.

"The heir doesn't have to play to be eaten," they answered.
Eight saints passed by,
                        eight green carved animals
                                and a goodlooking teller of tales.
When at last I opened my hand his face fell.
I had no intention of picking it up; it was talking off the floor.

XI

El joyero dormía cuando la octava niña retiró en anillo de
    bronce.
Ambos caballos buscaban jinete alrededor de la plaza;
otro caballo se alimentaba de crines bajo el árbol central.
Yo vaciaba mariposas negras para el extenso manto.
El caballero aceptó la espada y el perro ofrecidos por mí.
A no ser por la noche y mi propio canto hubiese quedado
    ciega.
Mi madre me llamó desde un balcón del sur.
Yo regresé con el pelo húmedo y los zapatos en la mano.

XI

The jeweler was asleep when the eighth girl took back the
    bronze ring.
Both horses were looking around the square for a rider;
another horse was feeding on manehair under the central tree.
I was excavating black butterflies for the outspread cloak.
The horseman took the sword and the dog I offered him.
To not be through night and my own song might have kept
    me blind.
My mother called me from a southern balcony.
I came back, skin damp, shoes in hand.

XII

Formaban grupos bajo un árbol sensible alternado
    azulmente.
Eran hombres con girasoles negros en lo más alto:
"Son cazadores, mártires y un gran orfebre; les pediré
    perdón."
Arrodillado confesé mi culpa pero no había juez.
Ninguno quería ser juez sin aves rosadas para confundirse.
La mujer que había sido hembra de reyes todavía llevaba
    corona.
"Le ofreceré un pájaro morado y esperaré sus órdenes."
Ayer por fin de la noche. Sólo los perros cambian de sitio.
Sólo los perros conocen mi girasol de la más pura tiniebla.

XII

They formed groups under a sensible tree turned bluish.
They were men with black sunflowers highest up:
"They are hunters, martyrs, a great silversmith; I will beg
their pardon."
Kneeling, I confessed my guilt but there wasn't any judge.
Nobody wanted to be judge without roseate birds to confuse
himself with.
The woman who had been the she of kings still wore her
crown.
"I offer you a purple bird and wait for your orders."
Yesterday, finally, night. Only the dogs move around.
Only the dogs have met my sunflower, purest abysmal black.

XIII

Alguna vez estaré en la ventana desconocida y seré la hija.
Pasará el acróbata largamente vestido de uno a otro cascabel;
de uno a otro cascabel cerrada de negro llevaré mi llanto.
La niña estará siempre en la montaña de muslos azules.
(Rescatad la Nación,
hacedle casa,

de su vientre han nacido los
pájaros
también la destrucción que llega a las altas mandíbulas.)
Haré la ronda con los niños tatuados: ésa es mi espalda;
pasará el hombre impulsado por su propia jauría: ése es mi
    rostro.
Allí donde su cabellera le dé muerte será la cita.

Iremos.

XIII

At some time I will be in the unknown window and I will be the
daughter.
The amply robed acrobat will pass from one rattlesnake to
another;
about one or another rattlesnake shut up in black I will lift up my
cry.
The girl will be always on blue thigh mountain.
(Rescue the Nation,
                        make it your house,
                                        out of your loins birds have been
                                        born,
as well as the destruction that comes to the tallest jawbones.)
I will court the tattooed children: that is my back;
the man will pass driven by his own wolfpack: that is my face.
There where his long hair may kill him will be the assignation.

We will go.

XIV

Madre, Madre, mi primo hermano pide noticias y lágrimas.
Le llevaré una lista de nacimientos (**tengo mala memoria**),
si el aroma perdura recordará la fruta ajustada a la última sed.
Yo quise que mi hijo no tuviera antifaz
pero un sol viril ha carcomido su rostro.
Madre, Madre, mi hijo yace flotando en un agua inmensa.
Anoche sus rodillas vacías recibiendo mis senos.
Desde mi cabecera, oh! madero infernal, comienza el túnel,
                    comienza la ascensión de rodillas.
Ordenes que obedezco: "Entregue sus pañuelos,
                    sus signos de puntuación,
                    su abecedario."
Frases sueltas: "Su cabellera será cortada en plenilunio."
La voz: "Estoy en deuda con el ciego que maltrata su bestia."

XIV

Mother, mother, my first cousin asks for news and tears.
I will take him a list of births (**my memory is bad**),
if the smell persists he will remember fruit fitted to ultimate
    thirst.
I wanted my boy not to have a mask
but a virile sun has chewed off his face.
Mother, mother, my boy lies afloat in an immense water.
Tonight his idle knees take my breasts in.
Behind my headboard, O! hellish timber, the tunnel begins,
                            the ascension begins of knees.
Orders I obey: "Give up your shawls,
                    your punctuation marks,
                    your ABCs."
Sentences let go of: "Your hair will be cut at full moon."
The voice: "I am kin to the blind man abusing his and your idiot."

« TERCER INTENTO DE CASA MATERNA »

Tercera medida, tercera entrega y tiempo para conseguir la casa.
Su plumaje que cubre el mes, que ensombrece muslo y cadera
    del año,
buen plumaje y entrecejo de amanecer cuando se fueron.
Recomendaciones: "Usted, isla; usted, mangle; usted, reina
    macaurel,
muy despacio y siempre con el girasol a la diestra."
Y ella que revisa todo, que zurce las roturas del cielo,
los desperfectos de la iguana y avanza muy despacio
por entre cortinajes de cera virgen claveteados en el otoño.

Tercer tiempo, tercera salida de las páginas
espantando el caballo blanco, orillando huesos de nube
brazos abiertos para no caerse. Y se distribuye el tiempo.
Se hacen paquetes y se colocan en los comercios humildes.
De tres en tres la tela, de tres en tres los metros de tela
con dibujos en el vientre, con labrantíos estampados sobre los
    muslos.

Por tercera vez (tercer intento de casa materna) se avanza, se
    avanza,
buscando quedarse, hacer fuego, quitar hollines de tiempo
    anterior,
reducir la flor al tamaño de lo eterno. Empeño solitario:
Usar el espejo para encerrar el águila. Oh! rosa de tinieblas
                      parada en la imagen del
                      sueño.

« THIRD TRY AT THE MOTHER HOUSE »

Third pacing it off, third giving it up, time now to get the house—
the plumage that covers the month, enshadows thigh and year-
    hip,
good plumage and sunrise-frown when they went away.
This is for your own good: "You, island; you, mangrove; you,
    queen cottonmouth,
go quite slow, sunflower at right hand always."
And she who scrutinizes everything, who sews up rips in the sky,
the iguana's flaws, and goes forward quite deliberately
between virgin beeswax draperies wearing studs in autumn.

Third time, third going out from the pages
spooking the white horse, embanking cloudbones,
arms open so as not to fall over themselves. And the time is doled
    out.
Packets are assembled and laid out in blue-collar trades.
Three by three the fabric, three by three the yards of fabric,
drawings on the belly, good farmland stamped on the thighs.

For the third time (third try at the mother house), forward,
    forward,
looking to stay put, to build a fire, to get rid of the smut of
    former time,
to reduce the blossom to the size of the eternal. A solitary pledge:
To use the mirror to shut the eagle up in. O! gloomrose
                                upright in the image
                                dreamed.

From *House Made of Utterance*   43

« RECADOS AL HERMANO MAYOR »

A Luis Daniel Terán

I

Los enlutados
que sonríen y pasan
dicen adiós con manos dobles.
Se apoyan en la frase del viejo prestigio familiar.
Para no avergonzarse, para no avergonzarse.
Pero se discute, se recuerda.
Hermanas mías, qué bellas fuimos.
Aún son bellas nuestras sombras.

« MESSAGES FOR THE OLDER BROTHER »

For Luis Daniel Terán

I

           The mourners
           who smile and pass by
           say goodbye with folded hands.
They ground themselves on the phrase of old family prestige.
Not to be ashamed, not to be ashamed.
But it is spoken of, it is remembered.
O my sisters, how lovely we were.
Our shadows are lovely still.

II

Compraron la noche, los errantes ligeros trajes del sueño,
la visita de piedra negra, sin lágrimas
cuando le dejaron eterno en su joven muerte.
Alguien compraba. Compraron fechas, nombres, rozaduras
    de plantas
sobre el pecho tan dulcemente expresivo de las niñas.
Compraron la casa, el árbol mío, muros, ladrillos,
puertas de cedro. También padre y madre. También nosotros
gente toda realmente hermosa, profunda, libre
afirmando el mismo fuego

                          la misma gracia de David
                          contra la torre anillada.

II

They bought the night, the wandering light dreamdresses,
the sight of black stone, without tears
when they left him evermore in his young death.
Somebody was buying. They bought dates, names, light
     touchings of plants
over the so sweetly affectionate breast of the girls.
They bought the house, my tree, walls, bricks,
cedar doors. Father and mother as well. Us as well,
folk all really handsome, deep, free
affirming the same fire

                         the same grace as David
                         facing the circled tower.

III

Casa mía, casa nuestra tantas veces pálida.
Semejante a esa flor que se hace oscura en la memoria
para luego volverse con otro rostro
                 desconociendo el sabor de las águilas
                     del pabellón sólo belleza,
todo de un golpe en el pecho del aire.
Y en este desprecio, hermano mío, en este desprecio.
Mi casa, nuestra casa de espalda a los bellos nombres,
majestuosa y sombría como a través de un mismo sueño;
reconocida y casi perfecta en núbiles rechazos
                en novia con su gajo de caña dulce
su pie desnudo, degollado sobre el césped floral.
La casa, la vieja casa del orgullo y de la violencia.

III

My house, our house, left pale so many times.
Like this flower that makes itself dark in memory
so as later to come back with another face
                    pretending not to know the taste of eagles
                            of beauty peculiar to the canopy
all at one strike in the air's breast.
And in this contempt, O my brother, in this contempt.
My house, our house, its rear to those handsome names,
majestic house and somber, as crossing through one selfsame
    dream,
recognized and almost perfect in nubile rejections,
                        in fiancée with stalk of sweet cane,
her naked foot's throat slit above flowering lawn.
The house, the old house of pride and raw force.

IV

Hubo perros como agujeros más oscuros en la sombra.
Inmensa extendida sobre el muro dibujaron el águila.
También números, perfiles, contorno de una mano izquierda.
Espuelas silenciadas:
altas estrechas rodillas de los capitanes agrarios.

IV

There were dogs like darker holes in the shade.
Immense, outspread, above the wall they sketched in the eagle.
Numbers too, profiles, outline of a left hand.
Muted spurs:
high narrow knees of agrarian captains.

Distante bella lobezna desprendida de los bosques;
inmensa y sombría como el descenso de las águilas
en la soledad de los salmos;
guardadora de verdades y máscaras opuestas
al rostro común señalado de infinito;
sensorial y eterna como el paso de las razas
sobre la brillantez oscura de las piedras;
miserable y a veces púdica
cuando la adolescencia razona el otoño
frente a las naciones fugitivas;
indestructible y casi perfecta
donde el hombre eleva sus ramos fúnebres
sus tazas ojerosas definitivamente castas,
donde los que se amaron ilustran la avenida de cada recuerdo,
de cada estación construyendo su casa fresca,
oscura en las riberas del poniente.
Inacabada espléndida mía que ordena y fija sus aves
en las sagradas visiones, que azuza enormes ligeras flores
contra la locura, su implacable vigilia,
que anda en sueños como la primavera en las alturas de la
    patria,
que hace oscura la fragancia del mar
                    de la noche sobre el reposo de los hartos.
Esta es tu casa, tu fogón de hierba húmeda
sobre las brasas de mi carne,
tu casa aún no mancillada por la gloria.
Roe pues tu creencia, tu madero interno,

« MUSIC WITH PSALM FOOT »

Handsome faraway she-wolf cub, turned loose in woods
immense and somber as eagles stooping
in psalm solitude;
caretaker of truths and masks at odds
with the common visage infinity indexed;
forevermore sensory as the tread is of bloodlines
over shining dark stones;
wretched and once in a while modest
when adolescence makes a case for fall
confronting nations on the run;
indestructible and nearly perfect
where the man lifts up his mortuary branches,
cups for haggard eyes distinctly chaste,
where self-loves light the way of each recollection,
of each season building a fresh house
dim on some western shore.
My splendid unfinished she-wolf who arranges birds and fixes
    them
in sacred visions, who urges on huge nimble blossoms
against skewed mind, pitiless vigil, who dream walks
the way spring does in native high ground,
and darkens the nocturnal sea-smell
                              over gluttonous repose.
This house is your house, your hearth of moist grass
above the hot coals of my flesh,
your house glory has not yet stained.
Gnaw then your credence, your internal timber,

tu sobriedad y antiguo paño sobre el relampagueo de mis huesos
y deja que interrumpa una vez más tu girasol
para regresar a mi rostro
para develar y bruñir aún más la puerta sombría de mis actos,
la sagacidad de los mármoles espaciados en el futuro.
Inacabada espléndida mía que anda en sueños
como la primavera en las alturas de la patria.

sobriety and antique fabric over the flashings of my bones,
and once again let your sunflower break in
and return to my face once again
to unveil and still further burnish the dreary doorway of my
     doings,
the sagacity of marble in future diffusion.
My splendid unfinished she-wolf who walks in dreams
the way spring does in native high ground.

« Piedrecillas de adivinación »

Como un océano, una claridad donde comienza el deseo.
Mucha, harta medida de escritura al paladeo total
o primer apunte de niñez que pudo ser salvado.
Esto y algo más de la frase: "La lluvia borró su carta."
Eternidad que se sucede sobre galayos de sequía sur.
Agua tres veces sentida en la palma de las manos.
Legados, copos de delicia señalando los tantos de cierta
    partida.
Esta pues, dulzura, mezclada con piedrecillas de adivinación.

Like an ocean, a clarity where longing gets started.
Much, a bellyful of writing to the entire palate
or first childhood memo that could be salvaged.
This and somewhat more from the phrase: "The rain erased your
note."
Eternity that happens over headlands of southern drought.
Water felt three times in the palm of the hand.
Legacies, cottonwads of delight betokening a tie in a certain match.
This then, pleasantness—all mixed up with pebbles for scrying.

« La poetisa cuenta hasta cien y se retira »

La poetisa recoge hierba de entretiempo,
pan viejo, ceniza especial de cuchillo;
hierbas para el suceso y las iniciaciones.
Le gusta acaso la herencia que asumen los fuertes,
el grupo estudioso, libre de mano y cerrado de corazón.
Quién, él o ella, juramentados, destinados al futuro:
Hijos de perra clamando tan dulcemente por el verbo,
implorando cómo llegar a la santa a su lenguaje de neblina.
Anoche hubo piedras en la espalda de una nación,
carbón mucho frotado en mejillas de aldea lejana.
Pero después dieron las gracias, juntaron, desmintieron,
retiraron junio y julio para el hambre. Que hubiese hambre.
La niña buena cuenta hasta cien y se retira.
La niña mala cuenta hasta cien y se retira.
La poetisa cuenta hasta cien y se retira.

« THE POETESS COUNTS TO 100 AND BOWS OUT »

The poetess gathers interim herbage,
aged bread, ash right for the knife,
herbs for the outcome and the first rites.
Maybe she likes the legacy the strong ones claim,
the studious group, hands free, hearts shut.
Who, he or she? oathbound, bound for the future:
Scions of a bitch baying so sweetly for the word, begging how
to get to the saint, her mistful tongue.
Last night there were stones on a nation's back,
much coal smeared on far village cheeks.
But then they gave thanks, shook hands, told some lies,
pulled back June and July for hunger. That there might be hunger.
The good girl counts to 100 and bows out.
The bad girl counts to 100 and bows out.
The poetess counts to 100 and bows out.

D E *Sonetos de todos mis tiempos*

« TANTO DE PAN, TANTO DE ACEITE »

Tanto de pan, tanto de aceite, tanto
de esto o de aquello, cálida medida
que aparta iguales trozos y salida
de percalas y láminas a tanto.

Dice: si miro recto y adelanto
un pie y luego el otro y con herida
mano alcanzo la flor no concedida
ni negociada por saber a cuanto,

entonces de qué vale hacer el trecho
diciendo adiós ya desgarrada el ala
"como en información de su derecho."

De qué vale la lluvia que resbala
por mejillas de jóvenes y pecho
de buena tierra que parece mala.

« SO MUCH BREAD, SO MUCH OIL »

So much bread, so much oil, so much
this or that, a piquant measure
that deals out just portions, lays out
effigies and percales just so.

She says: If I look straight ahead,
set one foot before the other,
and with hurt hand clutch the flower
neither yielded nor traded for,

then what's the use to make the stretch,
say goodbye, wing already ripped
"as informing you of your rights,"

what's the use of rainfall streaming
over young cheeks and over breast
of good earth that seems to be bad.

Los extraños llamaron a la puerta
para entregar caballos y monturas
de Chocontá, para entregar oscuras
polainas reflejando sobra yerta.

Reflejando en la página desierta
lo mejor de la vida y sus hechuras:
finas algarabías y cinturas
estrechas y muy jóvenes. Despierta

está la casa, la más niña pisa
como en sueños y en sueños la recibe,
espuela de oro que el amor conoce

sabiendo alzada palidez y risa.
La más joven la niña que concibe
camisa eterna de encendido roce.

« THE STRANGERS RATTLED AT THE DOOR »

The strangers rattled at the door
delivered horses and some gear
from Chocontá, delivered dark
chaparejos still new and stiff.

Showing on the deserted page
the best of vital handiwork:
lovely hubbub and fine youthful
lithe taut bellies. Now awake,

this house awake, the most youthful
girl-child dream-walks and in her dreams
meets it: the golden spur love knows

knowing uplifted pallid smile.
The youngest girl-child whose mind feels
merest friction of flaming shirt.

« Reconoció la noche en el espejo »

Reconoció la noche en el espejo
sin sospechar su rumbo ascendente.
Todo horizonte llega y de repente
el ave negra lanza su reflejo.

Rehúsa el corazón simple y complejo
conocer el final donde el presente
se vuelve recia oscuridad creciente
en torva lumbre y abisal reflejo.

Siente que el hado desmenuza el ala
que tuvo vuelo en el poniente escaso.
El ala sin país donde apoyarse.

Sin madre, sin espacio, sin escala
de amor como en el acto de salvarse.
El ala sola de encendido raso.

« SHE TOOK IN NIGHT IN THE PIER GLASS »

She took in night in the pier glass
unwary of its upward bent.
All horizons arrive, at once
the black bird launches its reflex.

Simply complex, the heart turns aside
from knowing the end where the now
becomes a robust darkness swelling
grim light into reflex abyss.

She feels destiny shred the wing
that took wing in a scrawny west,
wing with no land to set foot on.

No mother, no space, no stairway
love might clamber to safety on.
One solo satin wing in flames.

« HOJA ÚNICA, ERGUIDA MUY DESPACIO »

Hoja única, erguida muy despacio
sujeta a grises de encendida hartura,
hoja que mira y sabe de la obscura
fuerza del verde en reducido espacio.

Hoja de andar a tientas con reacio
lugar donde se afirma la moldura
de la brisa ciñendo bordadura
más clara en halo de cabello lacio.

Apresar un instante en la ventana
de ayer donde la especie relucía
con más hojas y un verde tan intenso

que la de hoy tan única y tan mía
es hoja de llegar y también pienso
hoja de hablar donde se para el día.

« ONE ONLY LEAF, ADAGIOED UP »

One only leaf, adagioed up
subject to grays of inflamed glut,
leaf that eyes and knows of the dark
might of green in whittled down space.

Leaf of groping self indulgent
stubborn place where the moulding holds
firm in a breeze girdling cross-stitch
clearer in an aura of lank hair.

To sieze a moment in the gone
window where the species is lighted
anew with leaves—with green so green

that this today so only mine
is a *here* leaf and I think too
a leaf of speech where day stands up.

Los moradores lanzan sus escritos
sobre pueblos, aldeas y ciudades.
Los moradores llevan sus crueldades
a destrozar la sombra de los mitos.

A ras de piso como en anteriores
hazañas y silbidos infinitos.
Documentos y pliegos manuscritos
a ras de piso por los corredores.

En la vigilia donde desempeña
el verbo amar su cometido puro,
los moradores hablan con alguna

muy precisa, buscando la reseña
de lo inaudito, hablando con alguna
que deslinda lo claro de lo obscuro.

« THEY WHO LIVE THERE HURL THEIR WRITINGS »

They who live there hurl their writings
at cities, villages, and towns.
They who live there lift feral rage
to ravage even ghosts of myths.

Razed to earth as in earlier
epic deeds and endless hisses.
Writs and folded manuscripts
along corridors razed to earth.

On the watch where the verb to love
unpawns its pure obligation,
they who live there speak with some she

quite precise, in search of the hint
at the unheard, speaking with her
who rives clarity out of cloud.

« En tus catorce versos surgen finas »

En tus catorce versos surgen finas
niña y mujer que fui, mas se engalana
puesta a ganar mi condición de anciana
como respuesta a tiempos que adivinas.

En tus catorce versos te confinas
para seguir con ella, por insana
ambición de quedar, húmeda plana
donde esmerada y púdica te afinas

para fungir en el primer terceto
de lengua brava, cálida lanceta
en estrechez clavada y recibida

en pleno rostro, oh! dardo que da vida.
Todas palabras doy en lumbre quieta
para vivir erguida en un soneto.

« SUBTLE IN YOUR FOURTEEN LINES SURGE »

Subtle in your fourteen lines surge
girl and woman I was, made up,
poised to be me now, an ancient,
reply to weathers you foresee.

You shut yourself in fourteen lines
to go on with her, through some mad
drive to remain, a yet wet page
where scrubbed and chaste you hone yourself,

unpawn self in the first tercet
of valorous tongue, fierce lancet
into tightness thrust and taken

full face on, O! shaft that gives life.
I give all words in noiseless light
to live, head high, in a sonnet.

« Una chenchena en el Suapure río »

Una chenchena en el Suapure río
sombría y recamada desde el vuelo
hasta el tazón de oscuro terciopelo
que devuelve la imagen del vacío.

Amontonado verde en el bajío;
tronco vivo que aviva mi recelo:
caimán de niebla hueca tras un velo
de indiferencia y abisal hastío.

Todo se mueve, pasa, queda afuera
de la estación, del año, del momento;
todo se aparta sin dañar la hora,

del alto, enamorado pensamiento.
Todo se restituye de manera
que el río pasa sin tocar el viento.

« IN THE SUAPURE RIVER »

In the Suapure River
a chenchena, grave, embroidered,
after flying to a black velvet bowl
becomes an icon of emptiness.

Green crowded up in the lagoon,
live tree-bole that fires suspicions:
croc from fog gap behind a scrim
of who cares, of blah bottomless.

All slides, goes by, remains outside
the season, year, moment; all moves
to one side, not bruising the hour,

the lofty smitten idea.
All comes back together to let
river pass without touching wind.

« ES UN CHARCO DE SOMBRA Y EN LA CARA »

Es un charco de sombra y en la cara
aire cruzaba almenas y cercados;
aire dejaba títulos morados
como si alguno en sueños se alejara.

Patria se enarca y lúcida se para
en sequías de Coro y arrancados
árboles que hemos visto arracimados
y a labores de viento dando cara.

Y a lo que fue y ha sido lo primero:
admirar equilibrio y mordedura
de verbo sin llegar; menos partida.

Verbo como de plomo en la bajura
del silábico modo que hace vida
en medio-tono gris del uno al cero.

« A PUDDLE OF SHADE, ON ITS FACE »

A puddle of shade, on its face
air crossing closes and battlements;
air was leaving purple titles
as if one will move off in dreams.

Homeland uprears and, lucid, gets
ready in Coro drought and ripped up
trees we have seen all in clusters
facing up to laboring wind.

And to what was and has been first:
to marvel at the poise and bite
of a verb not got; a minus entry.

A verb like a plumb bob in the deep
of a syllabic mode that makes life
in gray halftone from one to null.

« SABIDURÍAS DE TORZAL INCIERTO »

A Rimbaud

Sabidurías de torzal incierto
sobre linajes y cambios rosados;
tela urgida de tonos apagados
y multitud de corazón abierto.

Habla de dormitorios y de cierto
comedor donde madre y atajados
pájaros entre mallas apresados
para ser revendidos en el Puerto.

Cinturón que le dicen también faja
llena de morocotas. Hombre rico
despatarrado en calleja sombría.

Buenas piezas de holán y la baraja
marcada en la valija que traía:
Santo Lico del alma, Merolico.

« WISDOMS OF UNCERTAIN SILK CORDS »

To Rimbaud

Wisdoms of uncertain silk cords
over forebears and glozed changes,
weft urged on by colorless tones
and by a swarm with open heart.

You speak of bedrooms, and of one
dining room where sit a mother
and pent birds among coats of mail
siezed for resale at the harbor.

A belt said to be a money belt
full of gold dust. A filthy rich man
asprawl out in some dank alley.

Good bolts of linen and the marked
deck in the satchel he carried:
Saint Wolf of the soul, flimflammer.

« MÚSICA PARA LABIOS, TORBELLINO »

Música para labios, torbellino
en el fondo del piano; leve flauta
más allá del plumaje y de la incauta
melodía que ordena el desatino.

Aves enrumban vuelos a destino
de torzal enredado sin la pauta
del bajel que comanda el argonauta
con mano firme en igualdad de sino.

Cambios te asisten, músicas te atan
a hollines circulares como panas
de frente arriba y desprendido el fuego

de la paciencia y vuelven los que acatan
tu poesía Ana Enriqueta y sanas
del mal que aqueja tu presente ciego.

« MUSIC FOR LIPS, WHIRLWIND THE HEART »

Music for lips, whirlwind the heart
of the piano, flighty flute
out past plumage and incautious
air that arranges craziness.

Birds thrum into flights fated for
a silken snarl without the rule
the argonaut gave to his ship
with hand firm in ordained fairness.

Changes serve you, musics bind
to soots circular as velvets
on uplifted forehead and loosed

patient fire, they come back, those who
read your poems, Ana Enriqueta,
sane from what ails your eyeless now.

Las respuestas oscilan en un vano
asentir y la mano se dibuja
en la pared donde lo blanco empuja
y resuelve brilleces de verano.

Mucho le atañe afuera, con desgano,
pero aún así la flor se desdibuja
en estirada tela que repuja
aguja estable en inestable mano.

Acaso letras en arcano arribo
señalan arcos, rombos, animales
dulces al tacto como florecías

de espeso modo en ejemplar cultivo.
Abundancia de tintas y elegías
con hondo trecho de saberse vivo.

« THE REPLIES WAVER IN A VAIN »

The replies waver in a vain
assent and the hand is outlined
on the wall where white impresses,
resolves shining summer splashes.

Much outside frets you, dulls your taste,
still the bloom unsketches itself
on stretched cloth a steady needle
embroiders in unsteady hand.

Perhaps in arcane arrival
letters sign arcs, rhombs, animals
sweet to the touch like flowerets

from some dense mode of cultivar.
Hues and elegies aplenty,
deep stretch of knowing you're alive.

« NEGRO, AMARILLO, BLANCO COMO FINO »

*Elegía a un turpial que vivió y murió
en poder de la familia*

Negro, amarillo, blanco como fino
lugar del canto, pecho enarbolado
en fuegos, oros, pecho separado
en oscuros y claros, en divino

ardor como flechaje del destino
que aroma pico, resplandor parado;
un pulso como ramo enarbolado
por mano libre coloreando el trino.

Lumbre irascible, lumbre como caja
de pedrería que al amor se niega
siendo de amor la talla y la presencia.

El poeta consigue de la ausencia
nuevo caso de luz donde trasiega
un soneto que sirve de mortaja.

« BLACK, YELLOW, WHITE AS A SUBTLE »

Elegy for an oriole that lived and died
a captive of the family.

Black, yellow, white as a subtle
place in song, breast a flag in flames
flying golden, breast convening
obscures and clears, in a godlike

fervor like fated arrowings,
eager odor, idle splendor,
a pulse like a limb lifted high,
its free hand coloring a trill.

Furious light, light like a casket
of jewelry that love rejects,
being love's presence and tally.

The poet out of lack reaches
a new light-cask from which she draws
a sonnet serving her as shroud.

D E *Albatros*

F R O M *Albatross*

« ALBATROS »

Os piden dibujarlos en aires nuevos. Duermen en el aire.
Levitan en aires, distancias, acrecentados de humedad y
    pavura.
Abajo mares voltean sus fardos espesos,
su linfa gruesa de alevines y esporas,
su retorno a principios con densidad y textura de amor,
con acceso a núcleos brillantes
                    de **latidos futuros**.

« ALBATROSS »

They ask you to draw them in novel airs. They sleep in the
    air.
They levitate in airs, distances, accretions of damp and dread.
Undersea their loutish fardels tumble,
their lymph greasy with treacheries and spores,
their aboriginal returns dense with amorous texture,
accessing incandescent nuclei

                  of throbbings still to come.

« OFICIO ÁSPERO »

A R.P.S.

Para vuestra paz os ofrezco hoja rebrillando en lo oscuro;
sitio acodado en tarde humilde sometida a mi espejo
a mis hombros severamente anochecidos,
poblados de aves que pertenecen a luz distante: **también**
    vuestra luz.
Luz poderosa usada en meses vivos, en tactos vivos,
en sequías de oficio áspero sobre cotoperices y xerófilas,
sobre quietos cúmulos de aliento, no consolando,
                    solamente **no herir.**

« SPLINTERY RESPONSIBILITY »

To R.P.S.

For your peace I offer you a leaf newly shining in the dark;
a site bent over in late humble yielding to my mirror,
my severely benighted shoulders,
populous with birds proper to far-off light: **also your light**.
Potent light wielded in vital months, in vital touches,
in droughts of splintery responsibility over paddock-sages and
    sand-fleas,
over quiet breathing cumuli, not consoling, only
                              not to hurt.

Os sometieron. Labraron vuestro rostro con innumerables
   redes de edad.
                                        Irreconocible propio rostro.
Hicieron del albatros única señal en magnífica altura.
Oficiantes rehuían acercarse a obstinadas presencias.
Juventud y esplendor llevaban ánimos a desprendimiento
   absoluto.
Ahora se esquivan nuevos, engañosos lugares de sed
               espejuras de entorno para retomar lo perecedero.

« ASCENTS AND YET DISTANCES »

They threw you down. They scored your face with countless
    age networks.
                            You don't recognize your own face.
They made the albatross a singular sign magnificently aloft.
Celebrants kept their distance from those who looked stubborn.
Youth and splendor transported spirits to absolute indifference.
Now they avoid tricky new thirsty places—with mirrors all
    around
                            for tasting again what perishes.

« AVES NUNCA VISTAS »

Persona se afirma bajo follaje impredecible.
Sabe de árboles, mariposas, bayas picantes.
Sabe de bestias ocurridas en pampas, ambas (bestias, pampas)
                  sosegadas en aguas de corazón.
Ambas (bestias, pampas) como bajuras de pensamiento cauto.
                 Pero está el vuelo de aves nunca vistas.
Aves que existen. Aves como mesura y sentencia de lo blanco.
Aves pronunciadas por aquélla, acaso ya lejana en lados de acá
                donde aún se señala profundidad de latido.

« NEVER SEEN FOWL »

Somebody stands fast under unforespeakable leafery.
She knows of trees and butterflies, berries with bite.
She knows of dumb beasts come across on grassy plains, both
    (beasts and plains)
                         tranquilized in the heart's waters.
Both (beasts and plains) like careful thoughtful lowdown things.
                         But this is the flight of never seen fowl.
Fowl that are there. Fowl like the poise and judgment of blank.
Fowl uttered through what's maybe already way off on the sides
    of over here
                         where even throbdepth makes a signal of itself.

« TODAVÍA NO REPOSO »

Ultimos intentos de belleza.
R.F.B.

Reposar en no color, no aroma, tampoco caída o salvarse.
Iniciar descanso en ufanías de salud;
sufrimiento de rosa única vuelta hacia juventud, deseos,
    últimos intentos de belleza,
última, taciturna rosa-expresión ante un espejo recamado de
    propia imagen.
Imagen superpuesta a secuencia de escueto rango.
Rostro alguna vez cruzado por aves altísimas
como punto final de poema no escrito centrando la página

« NOT RESTING YET »

Beauty's last proposals
R.F.B.

To lie down in no color, no aroma, either downcast or to save
    yourself.
To initiate a workbreak, putting on healthy airs,
rosy forbearance, unique turn toward youth, yearnings, beauty's
    last proposals,
ultimate, taciturn rose-expression before a mirror cross-stitched
    with your own image.
Image overlaid on a sequence of unadorned rank.
Face at some time traversed by birds way high up
like the terminal point of an unwritten poem in the middle of
    a page

« VOLUNTAD DE GRITO RASGADO »

Tienen voz. Rayan tormentas con ásperos trazos de sonido.
Envuelven tinieblas y eluden exhalaciones de fuego azul.
Gozan de tempestades como creaturas de linaje sagrado.
Sinembargo fragor de noche no logra desunirlos.
Vuelan inmersos en círculos de protección y delicia.
Ala contra ala. Furioso persistir contra el rayo, su escritura en
    página negra
y como los ata, los envuelve con hilos de otra luz,
de otro, cegador nudo, que restaña sangre caliente.
Sangre, mancha de sangre creciendo en rasos, no porosos, no
    libres,
                sólo alas entre envergaduras de viento.

« WILL OF THE TORN SCREAM »

They have their say. They score torments with harsh sound
    scores.
They wrap up obscurities and elude blueflame outbreathings.
They exult in thunderstorms like creatures from sacred family
    trees.
Night's thunderous wreck will not manage to split them up
    anyway.
They fly merged in rapt protective circles.
Wing counters wing. Raving mad to keep on against jagged flash,
    scriven black page,
the flash bonds them, wraps them in other light fiber,
other bare blindness, stanching boiling blood.
Blood, bloody stain spreading out onto satins, not porous, not
    free,
                wings solo among stretched wingspans of wind.

D E *Autobiografía en tercetos*

FROM *Autobiography in Tercets*

« RÍO MOMBOY »

RÍO DE LA INFANCIA

> *En su camino beberá del torrente*
> *por eso levantará la cabeza.*
> Psalmo 109

La floración con su abundante cita
vence gajos, y lámina retoma
para encender lo blanco que suscita.

Paloma enfila su pesado aroma
de vuelo, en el follaje que se afina
hasta ser hueco y silbo de paloma.

Clamo por algún aire que defina
contornos en espuma, palma, rosa:
pequeño adorno en frente cristalina.

Paso de ser a estar, como dichosa
que anda entre sueños o talvez procura
probar en sueños fruta deliciosa,

viendo de lejos tallos de escritura
contra lo verde-azul, de arriba abajo,
asumidos colores y frescura.

Cuerpo enhebrado en oros y trabajo
de socavar el fondo, sin perjuicio
de brillos y pulidos a destajo.

« RÍO MOMBOY »

RIVER OF INFANCY

> *On his way he will drink from the stream;*
> *therefore he will lift up his head.*
> Psalm 110

Flowering lush annotation
whips torn limbs, retakes leaves,
firing up the white uprising.

A dove directs her weighty scent
down into leafage retuning
to dove's sibilant secure cave.

I clamor through air defining
surroundings of spume, palm tree, rose:
small gemstones on a glass-smooth brow.

I step from Be to Just Now Be,
glad dreamwalker making a way
to taste in dreams delicious fruit,

seeing way off scions of script
against bluegreen, from above below,
colors and freshness just put on.

Body threaded with gold, labor
undercutting rock bottom, no
quarrel with piecemeal rub and shine.

A cada instante ver el precipicio
de tu rumor y modos, con esmero
de quien se vierte en matinal oficio

de correr, aceptar rumbo primero.
Guárdame niña oh río de mi infancia.
Guarda este cetro donde vivo y muero.

Momboy asido a singular fragancia.

To see every moment the sheer
drop of murmur and modes, she pours
herself out with care in matins

to run and clasp the first plush show.
Keep me a girl, O infant stream:
Guard this realm I live and die in.

Momboy swathed in singular scent.

« EL MOTATÁN »

Es el poder del vuelco. Cesantía
de la dulzura. Pecho emancipado
con espacio de espuma en recia vía.

Desborda cauce, torso desgarrado.
Orillas yacen quietas y respiro
de arboledas profundas, con alado

canto, sulfilan el caliente giro
del follaje a consuno con umbroso
pulso de clima que, sumisa, admiro.

No de glareas puras el reposo
del fondo, si madeja sumergida
de reflejos en rueda. Fiero acoso.

Del borbollón y linfa decidida
resbala muslo. Abajo con la traba
de pedruzcos y rama sumergida.

Escojo de tu pecho lo que hallaba
mano inocente en tu lujoso frío,
por si la luz, inmensa, me acercaba

a peligroso círculo bravío.
(Gritos y risas en creciente enojo,
del recuerdo por húmedo extravío.)

« THE MOTATÁN »

Revolt boils over. Sweetness gets
the boot. Courage is given a free hand
in frothing space, on jagged way.

Torso flogged to tatters, you burst
out of bed, banks lie still, breathing
out deep groves of trees, winged cantos,

they stitch hot swirling leaves into
concord with a pulsing shadeful
climate I submit to admire.

The ground does not repose in pure
clear puddles if under water
reflexions snarl. Fierce, I go on.

From turbulent and determined lymph
a thigh slides off, goes down shackled
to boulder ruck, underwater bush.

I select from your stout heart what
innocence grasped in your lush cold,
in case some vast light brought me near

a feral circle. (Shouts and cries
and vexing laughter swell to break
through recollecting dank trespass.)

Misma esa luz, asida a trino rojo
de pájaro. Esa luz con filo tanto
que hirío, sajante, limpidez del ojo,

para dejar grabada en calicanto
fuente dichosa, en hora y hermosura,
con volantes de brisa y palosanto.

Tu mismo nombre, Motatán, figura
es de tumbos, caídas, levantarse
sonando fuerte en tajo. Desmesura.

Lo escrito, reposado, ha de salvarse
junto a tu nombre secular de río,
dispuesto a obedecer hasta dejarse

caer de golpe en tremedal sombrío.
Juventud mía estuvo en tu corriente.
Escúdame en tu pecho. Tú en el mío.

Y dame ser eterna en tu presente.

This same light, clutching at a bird's
red trill. This light so very keen
it hurt, sliced a limpid eye to leave

in some stonemason's wall a glad
fountain, in good time, good looking,
with frilly airs and guitar trees.

Just your name, Motatán, calls up
tombs, cataclysms, lifts you high,
blares might from sheer crag. Too much might.

What's scored, at rest, must save itself
bound to the common word *river*,
poised to obey until it falls

thunderclapping into a bog.
I spent my girlhood in your stream.
Keep me in your heart, you in mine.

Make me eternal in your now.

« Otros Ríos »

Neverí, Manzanares, El Cabriales
de Braulio Salazar, pintor amigo
quieto en su nombre: ámbitos cabales

de grandeza, por ser fino testigo
del río moribundo, su poeta
en líneas y color. Apenas digo

de este río, sin oros y sin meta.
El, que otrora feliz, hizo a destajo
inmenso cauce en la planicie neta.

Yo me vuelvo al Burate donde encajo
ya con vejez al hombro. Tenebrosa
de tanta luz, que sin moverme, atajo,

y devuelvo al aroma de la rosa.
Por nieblas y peñascos se avecina
Orlando Araujo, frente milagrosa

conocido de mí, por letra endrina
y espuma de sus ríos; cambio y grado
de nostalgia con piel de mandolina.

El Jiménez ahora. Su dictado
de tropicales giros. Su contienda
de pájaros, y bosque conquistado.

<< OTHER RIVERS >>

Neverí, Manzanares, El
Cabriales, a dying stream
attested to in fine faultless

grand tours by Braulio Salazar,
painter friend wearing tranquil name,
poet working color and line.

I scarcely speak of it, it has
no golds, no finish line. Once
tirelessly happy, it laid down

a great gash in prime bottomland.
I go back to the Burate
where presently I wrap some age

around my shoulders. This much light
fills me so full of gloom I take
a shortcut leading me, unmoved,

to rose aroma one more time.
Through mists and boulders, Orlando
Araujo nears me, fabulous

forehead I know through reading sloe
script and riverspume, nostalgia's
change and grade in mandolin skin.

Castán de hoy. Secreto me defienda
de alguna púa ingente, pues la suma
de cuanto fuí no quiero que se entienda

si nó después de ser escueta ruma
de versos, de espirales a lo ignoto
como de río desguazando espuma.

El Chama, su sollozo grís anoto.
Aún con vida sus pulsos abisales.
El Chama, gran rumor de pecho roto,

cayendo en sucios canjes terrenales.
Sálvate río, sálvame y resiste
pues nuestras soledades son iguales.

¡Nunca, tanta de amor ardido, viste!

The Jiménez now, dictating
tropical swirls, stirring up
quarrelsome birds, woods lost to siege.

Today's Castán. Secrecy keeps
me from being run through: The sum
of what I was I do not want

known unless I can then be bare
verse-heaps spiring out of mind
the way a river unmakes spume.

The Chama: I score its drab sob,
even the abyss pulses with life.
Chama, grand murmur of burst breast,

falling in filth as the world turns.
Save yourself, river, and me: Keep on:
Our isolations are the same.

You've never known such glowing love!

« Invocación a la madre »

Es tanta soledad, soledad tanta
como del ave que acrecienta altura
y traspasa la luz y la quebranta

para invocar respiración futura
y paso a paso sofrenar el grito
hasta hacer de la piedra, su andadura.

Endurecer el aire; lo finito
asido con firmeza, de manera
que lo uno ni lo otro formen mito

y si la madre como voz primera,
audible, pero llena del momento
donde se unen el fuego y la madera.

Donde se unen defensa y pensamiento.
De piedra la andadura y saber fuerte
que, en sus brazos, la piedra fué lamento

y recibe con ambito de muerte
la que fué niña suya, sin descanso
y sigue siendo suya, de tal suerte

que jamás la dulzura hizo remanso
en trato igual, de dos que fueron una:
ambas de soledad y pliego canso.

« INVOCATION TO THE MOTHER »

As much solitude, solitude
as much as bird that hefts her height
and pierces light and smashes it

to call for future breath, and step
by step to hold the shout in check
until her going turns to stone.

The air made solid; the finite
clung to so tightly neither one
nor the other may take form as myth

and if as mother, then as first
earful, filled with the moment when
flaming and wood turn into one.

Where fence and thought turn into one.
The stony going and mighty thought
that in their arms the stone was woe

and you receive, strolling with death,
what was your daughter, with no break,
and goes on being yours, so that

sweetness never built a haven
in fair deal struck by two made one:
two solitudes and a slack writ.

Pliego donde dispuso la fortuna
estrellarse, llegar, hacer del grito
nube de tacto o clámide de luna.

Porque ella espera en el secreto rito
del saludo. La Madre, su semilla
su "defender" de cara al infinito.

Entonces, pues, recibirá sencilla
labia, para que el pecho donde crezca
sea como de trigo a la rodilla.

Y hará que con la luz desaparezca
todo temor, toda esperanza vana
que un dulce giro de salir, ofrezca.

O se lleve de frente la mañana
con su hervor de reseda, conseguida
a fuerza de ceñir cielo y campana.

(Porque no he de salir, enfebrecida,
a retomar la pálida congoja
de, sin bandera, atravesar la vida.)

Mostrar el corazón hoja por hoja,
para no ser mirado, pues lo nuevo,
ni quién lo escuche, o ruede, o lo recoja.

A tanta soledad pido relevo.
Ser libre al fondo, al lado, en primer plano.
O recostarse donde no me atrevo.

Madre utiliza símbolos y en vano
quiero desentrañar oscura data
de quien invita y no me dá la mano.

Writ where hazard brought into play
a starburst, to arrive, transform
tact into cloud or lunar cloak.

She puts her hope in the dark rite
of robust health. The Mother's seed
her "face saver" to the last gasp.

Then (then) she'll receive the simple
lip, so the bosom it grows at
may be like knee-high standing wheat.

She'll behave so that with the light
all fear will fade, all empty hope
a sweet gyre of going offers.

Or maybe lift her brow toward morning
with reseda warmth, got hold of
by buckling up parish and sky.

(Because I don't need to go, weak,
to drink again the pallid grief
of marching through life with no flag.)

To lay the heart bare, leaf by leaf,
not to be looked at because new,
given ear to, rolled over, reaped.

I want relief from solitude.
To be free at bottom, side, front.
Or to lie down where I don't dare.

Mother uses symbols; in vain
I dig through guts for dark data:
who invites and doesn't shake hands.

A este idioma seguro no lo ata
ninguna indecisión, pues lanza fino
dardo de libertad. Así rescata

parte de sombra y parte de destino.
Es difícil decir algo que oprime
y no salirse un tanto del camino

de ser. El verbo clave no me exime
de estar. Estoy aquí. Punto y extremo
de ave, que me dispara y me redime.

Ave **madre**. Poder. Impulso. Remo
en esta calma, sin rizada altura
y no por no saber, ni porque temo

como algún otro, ciega investidura
llamando desde clámide remota.
Es tu **hija** en su noche "siempre oscura."

Noche del alma que en silencio acota,
para seguir después en alta frente
ignorando desguazo y ala rota

que anotaré, mañana en nueva fuente.

To this sure idiom is fastened no
quibble at all; I throw a keen
freedom dart. That's how it rescues

part from shadow and part from fate.
It's hard to say what grinds you down
and not veer too much off the way

of Being. *Key* won't set me free
from Being. Here. Point and utmost
of bird that shoots me and goes my bail.

Mother bird. Might. Drive. I paddle
on this calm unwrinkled surface,
not through not knowing, not fearing,

as if someone else, a blind call
after some far-off manly cloak. It's your
daughter, in her "ever dark" night.

Night of soul that, silent, marks off,
to follow later with head high,
ignoring wreck and broken wing,

what I will score: new day, new source.

THE LOCKERT LIBRARY OF POETRY IN TRANSLATION

George Seferis: Collected Poems (1924–1995), translated, edited, and introduced by Edmund Keeley and Philip Sherrard

Collected Poems of Lucio Piccolo, translated and edited by Brian Swann and Ruth Feldman

C. P. Cavafy: Selected Poems, translated by Edmund Keeley and Philip Sherrard and edited by George Savidis

Benny Andersen: Collected Poems, translated by Alexander Taylor

Selected Poetry of Andrea Zanzotto, edited and translated by Ruth Feldman and Brian Swann

Poems of René Char, translated and annotated by Mary Ann Caws and Jonathan Griffin

Selected Poems of Tudor Arghezi, translated by Michael Impey and Brian Swann

"The Survivor" and Other Poems by Tadeusz Różewicz, translated and introduced by Magnus J. Krynski and Robert A. Maguire

"Harsh World" and Other Poems by Angel González, translated by Donald D. Walsh

Ritsos in Parentheses, translations and introduction by Edmund Keeley

Salamander: Selected Poems of Robert Marteau, translated by Anne Winters

Angelos Sikelianos: Selected Poems, translated and introduced by Edmund Keeley and Philip Sherrard

Dante's "Rime," translated by Patrick S. Diehl

Selected Later Poems of Marie Luise Kaschnitz, translated by Lisel Mueller

Osip Mandelstam's "Stone," translated and introduced by Robert Tracy

The Dawn Is Always New: Selected Poetry of Rocco Scotellaro, translated by Ruth Feldman and Brian Swann

Sounds, Feelings, Thoughts: Seventy Poems by Wisława Szymborska, translated and introduced by Magnus J. Krynski and Robert A. Maguire

.The Man I Pretend to Be: "The Colloquies" and Selected Poems of Guido Gozzano, translated and edited by Michael Palma, with an introductory essay by Eugenio Montale

D'Après Tout: Poems by Jean Follain, translated by Heather McHugh

Songs of Something Else: Selected Poems of Gunnar Ekelöf, translated by Leonard Nathan and James Larson

The Little Treasury of One Hundred People, One Poem Each, compiled by Fujiwara No Sadaie and translated by Tom Galt

The Ellipse: Selected Poems of Leonardo Sinisgalli, translated by W. S. Di Piero

The Difficult Days by Roberto Sosa, translated by Jim Lindsey